Contents

GW00866106

Name: _____

1 Small letters

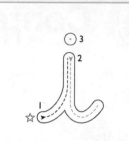

Write over each *i* on the line here.
Start at the ☆.

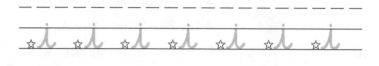

Now practise writing the letter *i* .

Tiger Tim is feeling ill.

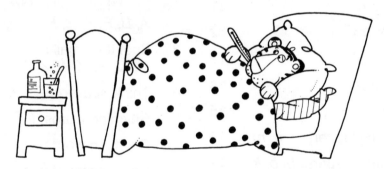

How many times is *i* used in the sentence?

Practise writing over the letter *i* in these words.

in   is   it   ill   dip   mini

in   is   it   ill   dip   mini

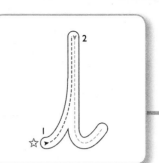

Write over each l on the line here.
Start at the ☆.

Now practise writing the letter l .

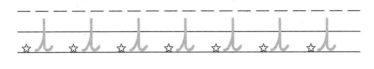

All lions like to lunch.

How many times is l used in the sentence?

Practise writing over the letter l in these words.

leg lip little ball fell

leg lip little ball fell

3

3 Small letters

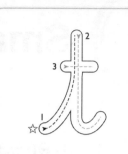

Write over each *t* on the line here.
Start at the ☆.

☆*t*   ☆*t*   ☆*t*   ☆*t*   ☆*t*   ☆*t*

Now practise writing the letter *t*.

☆   ☆   ☆   ☆   ☆   ☆   ☆   ☆   ☆   ☆   ☆

Tom tries trampolining.

How many times is *t* used in the sentence? [ ]

Practise writing over the letter *t* in these words.

tip   try   two   tall   attic   get

tip   try   two   tall   attic   get

4

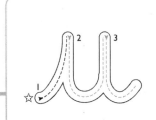

Write over each ‿ on the line here.
Start at the ☆.

Now practise writing the letter ‿ .

Huddle under the umbrella.

How many times is ‿ used in the sentence?

Practise writing over the letter ‿ in these words.

up us under cup run

up us under cup run

5 Small letters

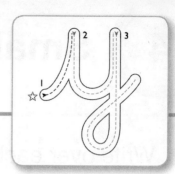

Write over each y on the line here.
Start at the ☆.

Now practise writing the letter y .

☆   ☆   ☆   ☆   ☆   ☆   ☆   ☆   ☆   ☆   ☆

A yellow yak yawns.

How many times is y used in the sentence? ☐

Practise writing over the letter y in these words.

you yo-yo eye fly my

you yo-yo eye fly my

6) Small letters

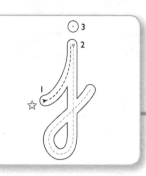

Write over each *j* on the line here.
Start at the ☆.

☆*j* ☆*j* ☆*j* ☆*j* ☆*j* ☆*j* ☆*j* ☆*j*

Now practise writing the letter *j* .

☆   ☆   ☆   ☆   ☆   ☆   ☆   ☆   ☆   ☆   ☆

John enjoys jogging.

How many times is *j* used in the sentence? [ ]

Practise writing over the letter *j* in these words.

jig jug joke jump enjoy

jig jug joke jump enjoy

Practising small letters

_i_ _l_ _t_

Write each of the letters on the three lines below.
Start at the ☆.

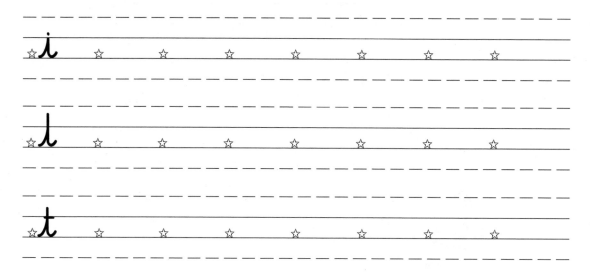

Now practise writing the three letters again by writing
over the grey letters in each of the words below.

ill ill   _lit lit_

till till   _will will_

fall fall   _belt belt_

milk milk   _laugh laugh_

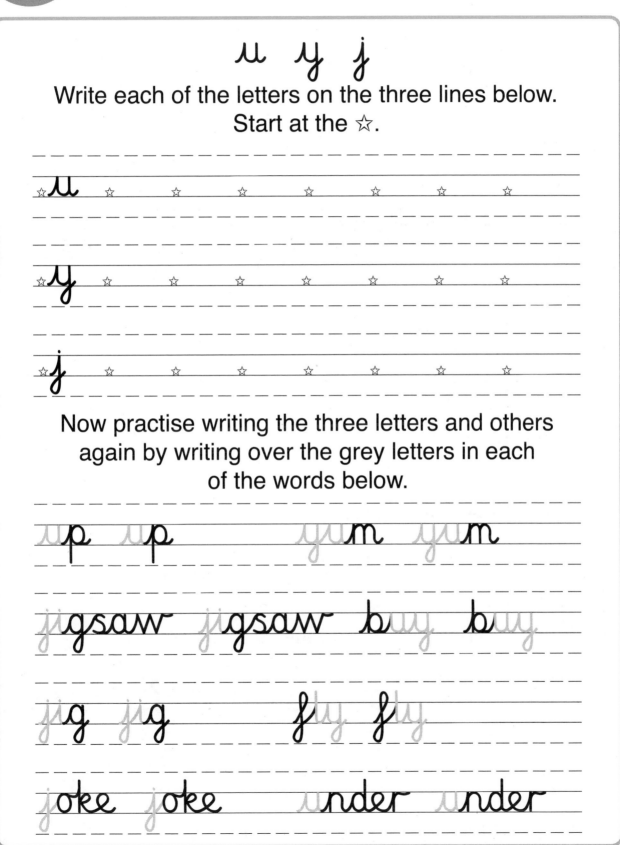

u y j

Write each of the letters on the three lines below.
Start at the ☆.

Now practise writing the three letters and others
again by writing over the grey letters in each
of the words below.

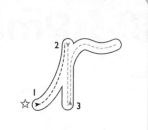

Write over each 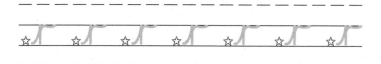 on the line here.
Start at the ☆.

Now practise writing the letter ⌐ .

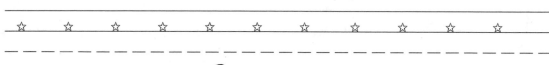

Robby rabbit runs around.

How many times is ⌐ used in the sentence?

Practise writing over the letter ⌐ in these words.

rip rat roll b rin car fur

rip rat roll b rin car fur

10 Small letters

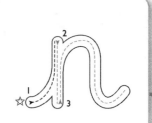

Write over each ⌒ on the line here.
Start at the ☆.

Now practise writing the letter ⌒.

Nine hens running.

How many times is ⋂ used in the sentence?

Practise writing over the letter ⌒ in these words.

no nap not bend pin

no nap not bend pin

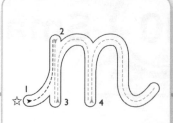

Write over each m on the line here.
Start at the ☆.

☆m ☆m ☆m ☆m ☆m

Now practise writing the letter m.

☆   ☆   ☆   ☆   ☆   ☆   ☆   ☆   ☆

Making music on a motorbike.

How many times is m used in the sentence?

Practise writing over the letter m in these words.

me my mum lump am

me my mum lump am

12 Small letters

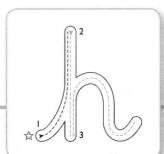

Write over each *h* on the line here.
Start at the ☆.

Now practise writing the letter *h* .

☆   ☆   ☆   ☆   ☆   ☆   ☆   ☆   ☆   ☆   ☆

Happy horses eating hay.

How many times is *h* used in the sentence?

Practise writing over the letter *h* in these words.

her him have chop fish

her him have chop fish

Write over each *b* on the line here.
Start at the ☆.

Now practise writing the letter *b* .

☆   ☆   ☆   ☆   ☆   ☆   ☆   ☆   ☆   ☆   ☆

Branches bend in the breeze.

How many times is *b* used in the sentence?

Practise writing over the letter *b* in these words.

by but bull about tub

by but bull about tub

14 Small letters

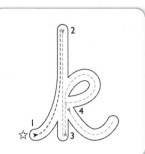

Write over each _k_ on the line here.
Start at the ☆.

☆k ☆k ☆k ☆k ☆k ☆k

Now practise writing the letter _k_ .

☆ ☆ ☆ ☆ ☆ ☆ ☆ ☆ ☆ ☆ ☆

Kangaroos like kicking.

How many times is _k_ used in the sentence? ▢

Practise writing over the letter _k_ in these words.

keep kiss lick like tick

keep kiss lick like tick

⬤ 15 Practising small letters

r n m

Write each of the letters on the three lines below.
Start at the ☆.

Now practise writing the three letters and others
again by writing over the grey letters in each
of the words below.

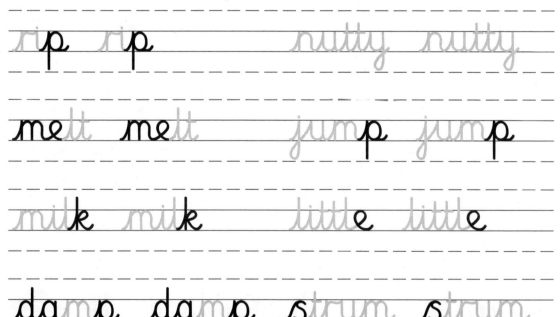

h b k

Write each of the letters on the three lines below.
Start at the ☆.

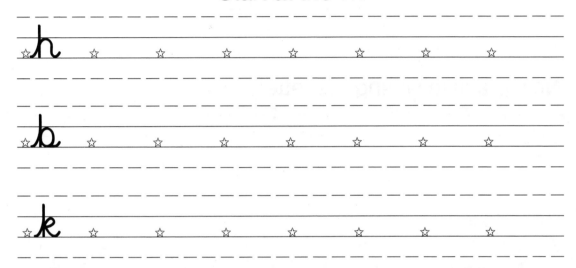

Now practise writing the three letters and others
again by writing over the grey letters in each
of the words below.

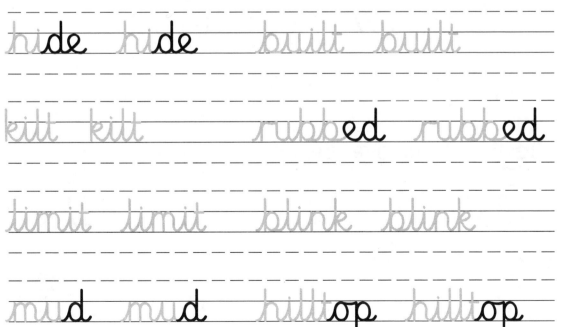

Small letters

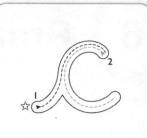

Write over each c on the line here.
Start at the ☆.

☆c ☆c ☆c ☆c ☆c ☆c

Now practise writing the letter c.

☆   ☆   ☆   ☆   ☆   ☆   ☆   ☆   ☆   ☆   ☆

Count the cuddly cats.

How many times is c used in the sentence?

Practise writing over the letter c in these words.

cut call chick reach attic

cut call chick reach attic

Small letters

Write over each _o_ on the line here.
Start at the ☆.

☆_o_ ☆_o_ ☆_o_ ☆_o_ ☆_o_ ☆_o_

Now practise writing the letter _o_ .

☆ ☆ ☆ ☆ ☆ ☆ ☆ ☆ ☆ ☆ ☆

Owls hoot at the moon.

How many times is _o_ used in the sentence?

Practise writing over the letter _o_ in these words.

on out over how go

on out over how go

19 Small letters

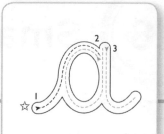

Write over each *a* on the line here.
Start at the ☆.

Now practise writing the letter *a* .

☆   ☆   ☆   ☆   ☆   ☆   ☆   ☆   ☆   ☆   ☆

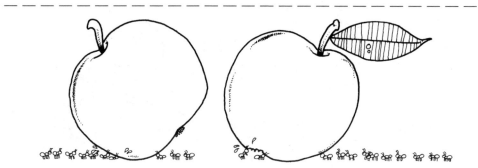

Ants like eating apples.

How many times is *a* used in the sentence?

Practise writing over the letter *a* in these words.

am   as   are   hat   back   era

am   as   are   hat   back   era

20 Small letters

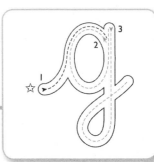

Write over each *g* on the line here.
Start at the ☆.

Now practise writing the letter *g*.

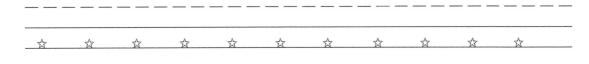

Eight bottles of gooey glue.

How many times is *g* used in the sentence?

Practise writing over the letter *g* in these words.

go get grin age leg peg

go get grin age leg peg

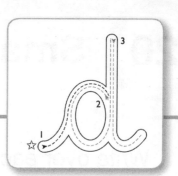

Write over each d on the line here.
Start at the ☆.

d d d d d d

Now practise writing the letter d .

Dinosaurs dancing daintily.

How many times is **d** used in the sentence?

Practise writing over the letter d in these words.

do   dog   edge   hid

do   dog   edge   hid

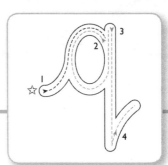

Write over each q on the line here.
Start at the ☆.

Now practise writing the letter q.

The Queen queues quietly.

How many times is q used in the sentence?

Practise writing over the letter q in these words.

quit quack quiet liquid

quit quack quiet liquid

Practising small letters

c o a

Write each of the letters on the three lines below.
Start at the ☆.

☆ c ☆ ☆ ☆ ☆ ☆ ☆ ☆

☆ o ☆ ☆ ☆ ☆ ☆ ☆ ☆

☆ a ☆ ☆ ☆ ☆ ☆ ☆ ☆

Now practise writing the three letters and others
again by writing over the grey letters in each
of the words below.

care care oats oats

acorn acorn blame blame

roam roam closed closed

ape ape orange orange

Write each of the letters on the three lines below.
Start at the ☆.

Now practise writing the three letters and others
again by writing over the grey letters in each
of the words below.

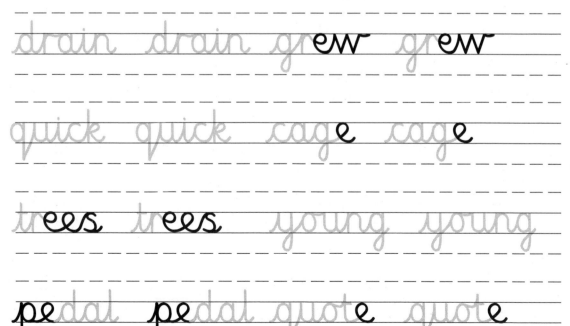

25

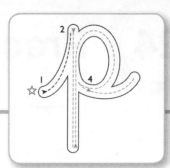

Write over each ρ on the line here.
Start at the ☆.

☆ ρ ☆ ρ ☆ ρ ☆ ρ ☆ ρ ☆ ρ

Now practise writing the letter ρ .

☆   ☆   ☆   ☆   ☆   ☆   ☆   ☆   ☆   ☆   ☆

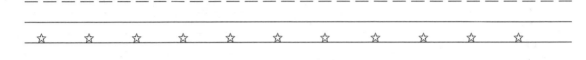

A pirate paints a paddle.

How many times is ρ used in the sentence?

Practise writing over the letter ρ in these words.

pet put pull rope top chip

pet put pull rope top chip

Write over each ℓ on the line here.
Start at the ☆.

☆ℓ ☆ℓ ☆ℓ ☆ℓ ☆ℓ ☆ℓ

Now practise writing the letter ℓ.

☆   ☆   ☆   ☆   ☆   ☆   ☆   ☆   ☆   ☆   ☆

Elaine eats eleven eggs.

How many times is ℓ used in the sentence? ☐

Practise writing over the letter ℓ in these words.

eat   end   over   see   send

eat   end   over   see   send

27 Small letters

Write over each *s* on the line here.
Start at the ☆.

s s s s s s s s s s s s

Now practise writing the letter *s* .

☆   ☆   ☆   ☆   ☆   ☆   ☆   ☆   ☆   ☆   ☆

A sailing ship at sea.

How many times is *s* used in the sentence?

Practise writing over the letter *s* in these words.

so   say   sell   house   kiss

so   say   sell   house   kiss

Write over each _f_ on the line here.
Start at the ☆.

Now practise writing the letter _f_.

Frogs flicking Frisbees.

How many times is _f_ used in the sentence?

Practise writing over the letter _f_ in these words.

fin fly for raft if tiff

fin fly for raft if tiff

29 Small letters

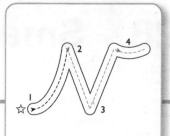

Write over each $\mathcal{N}$ on the line here.
Start at the ☆.

☆$\mathcal{N}$ ☆$\mathcal{N}$ ☆$\mathcal{N}$ ☆$\mathcal{N}$ ☆$\mathcal{N}$ ☆$\mathcal{N}$

Now practise writing the letter $\mathcal{N}$.

☆   ☆   ☆   ☆   ☆   ☆   ☆   ☆   ☆   ☆   ☆

Five movers in a van.

How many times is $\mathcal{N}$ used in the sentence?

Practise writing over the letter $\mathcal{N}$ in these words.

nain very ever cover wave

nain very ever cover wave

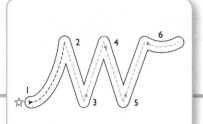

Write over each  on the line here. Start at the ☆.

Now practise writing the letter ⅏.

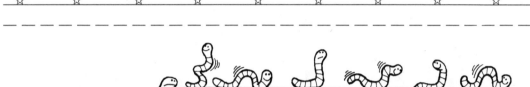

Wobbly worms on a wall.

How many times is ⅏ used in the sentence? ☐

Practise writing over the letter ⅏ in these words.

we why when two bow

we why when two bow

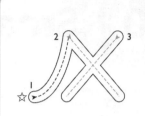

Write over each  on the line here.
Start at the ☆.

Now practise writing the letter  .

Six foxes in boxes.

How many times is ✗ used in the sentence?

Practise writing over the letter  in these words.

fix   mix   axe   flex   coax

fix   mix   axe   flex   coax

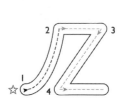

Write over each _z_ on the line here.
Start at the ☆.

☆_z_ ☆_z_ ☆_z_ ☆_z_ ☆_z_ ☆_z_

Now practise writing the letter _z_.

☆   ☆   ☆   ☆   ☆   ☆   ☆   ☆   ☆   ☆   ☆

Dozy zebras in the zoo.

How many times is _z_ used in the sentence?

Practise writing over the letter _z_ in these words.

zip zero glaze buzz fizz

zip zero glaze buzz fizz

33 Practising small letters

Write each of the letters on the three lines below.
Start at the ☆.

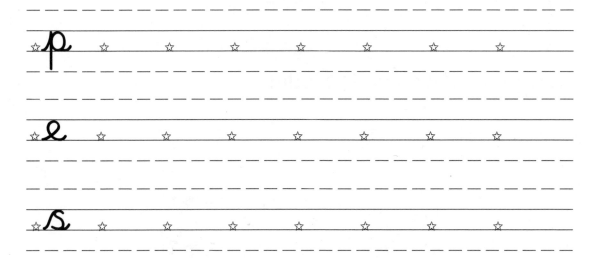

Now practise writing the three letters and others
again by writing over the grey letters in each
of the words below.

f v w

Write each of the letters on the three lines below.
Start at the ☆.

☆f ☆   ☆   ☆   ☆   ☆   ☆   ☆

☆v ☆   ☆   ☆   ☆   ☆   ☆   ☆

☆w ☆   ☆   ☆   ☆   ☆   ☆   ☆

Now practise writing the three letters and others
again by writing over the grey letters in each
of the words below.

fact fact   vase vase

whizz whizz   half half

cover cover   slow slow

wash wash   quiz quiz

Practising small letters

x   z

Write each of the letters on the three lines below.
Start at the ☆.

☆x   ☆   ☆   ☆   ☆   ☆   ☆   ☆

☆z   ☆   ☆   ☆   ☆   ☆   ☆   ☆

Now practise writing the two letters and others
again by writing over the grey letters in each of
the words below.

wax wax   zebra zebra

mixed mixed lazy lazy

boxer boxer   puzzle puzzle

pixie pixie   buzz buzz

Small letters can be written in many different styles, which can make them look like other letters. In the boxes, draw a line between each capital letter and the correct small letters.

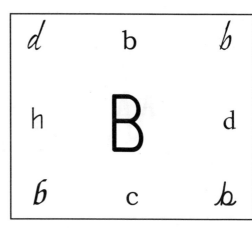

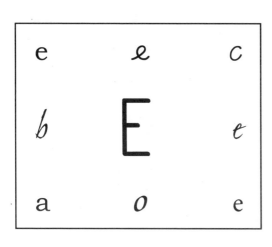

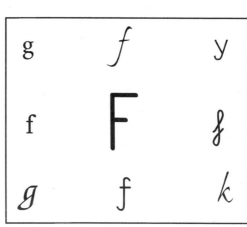

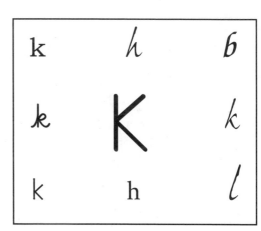

37 Spot the small letters

Small letters can be written in many different styles, which can make them look like other letters. In the boxes, draw a line between each capital letter and the correct small letters.

n	m	m
n	M	n
m	m	w

q	p	g
q	Q	q
g	p	q

s	z	s
z	S	x
s	z	s

u	v	v
w	V	u
v	v	w

u	v	w
w	W	w
u	w	v

z	a	z
z	Z	x
z	s	s

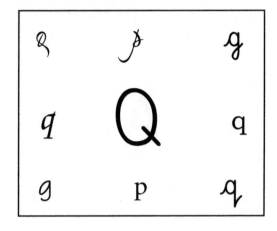

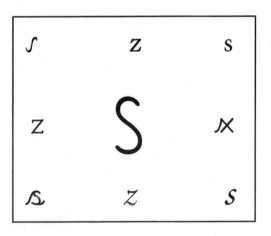

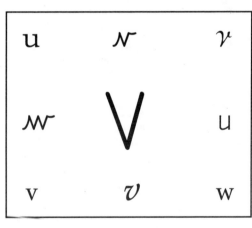

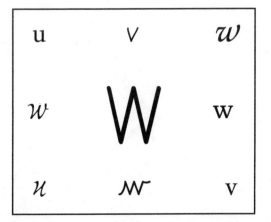

Think of a word

Can you write a word beginning with each
of the letters in the alphabet?
Some have been done for you.

a is for _apple_

b is for _b_

c is for _c_

d is for _d_

e is for _egg_

f is for _fish_

g is for _g_

h is for _h_

i is for _insect_

j is for _j_

k is for _kids_

l is for _l_

m is for _m_

n is for _n_

o is for _o_

p is for _p_

q is for _queen_

r is for _r_

s is for _s_

t is for _t_

u is for _umbrella_

v is for _very_

w is for _w_

x is for _x-ray_

y is for _y_

z is for _z_

39 Rhyming words

Write each of the words below. Start at the ☆.
When you have finished, read the words
aloud to your partner.

lit

bit

hit

sit

wit

fit

grit

Write each of the words below. Start at the ☆.
When you have finished, read the words
aloud to your partner.

hill

pill

will

mill

grill

fill

bill

Rhyming words

Write each of the words below. Start at the ☆.
When you have finished, read the words
aloud to your partner.

bin

tin

grin

fin

win

din

pin

Rhyming words

Write each of the words below. Start at the ☆.
When you have finished, read the words
aloud to your partner.

☆tip ☆ ☆ ☆ ☆ ☆

☆rip ☆ ☆ ☆ ☆ ☆

☆whip ☆ ☆ ☆

☆zip ☆ ☆ ☆ ☆ ☆

☆pip ☆ ☆ ☆ ☆ ☆

☆drip ☆ ☆ ☆ ☆

☆grip ☆ ☆ ☆ ☆

Rhyming words

Write each of the words below. Start at the ☆.
When you have finished, read the words
aloud to your partner.

lick

kick

stick

thick

brick

flick

pick

Write each of the words below. Start at the ☆.
When you have finished, read the words
aloud to your partner.

☆wing

☆ring

☆sting

☆sing

☆fling

☆bring

☆king

Rhyming words

Write each of the words below. Start at the ☆.
When you have finished, read the words
aloud to your partner.

dig

big

pig

wig

fig

twig

rig

Write this well-known rhyme in your
best handwriting. When you have finished,
read it aloud to your partner.

Jack and Jill went up the hill

To fetch a pail of water;

Jack fell down and broke his crown,

And Jill came tumbling after.

Write this well-known rhyme in your best handwriting. When you have finished, read it aloud to your partner.

Hey, diddle, diddle!

The cat and the fiddle,

The cow jumped over the moon;

The little dog laughed

To see such fun,

And the dish ran away with the spoon.